MarkTruth™

The Truth About Self-Publishing Your Book

WORKBOOK

Developed by Mark T. Arsenault

Copyright 2017 by Mark T. Arsenault. All rights reserved. No portion of this book may be reproduced in any format without written permission, except for use allowable under U.S. copyright law. ISBN-10: 1-890305-31-6, ISBN-13: 978-1-890305-31-4. *MarkTruth*, *MarkTruth.com* and *The Truth About Self-Publishing Your Book* are trademarks owned by Mark T. Arsenault. Visit **MarkTruth.com** for tons of free inspirational, motivational and instructional material.

"I write books to influence people I will never meet. Books increase my audience and my message."

—*Les Parrot*

Top 10 Reasons to Self-Publish Your Book

1. Maintain Complete _____ of Your Book

When we create something it's like _____ _____ to it.

2. Retain the _____ to Your Work

Lost rights could mean a lot of lost _____.

3. Get Your Book Published _____

It's possible to have your book available to buy in less than _____ _____.

4. Earn More _____

Authors earn _____ (a percentage of book sales).

Authors earn _____% of the price of their *Kindle* books for each sale.

5. Get Paid _____

Authors sometimes weren't paid for _____ after sale of a book!

Electronic book sales can be tracked in virtual _____ _____.

6. Take Advantage of Trends

_____ of Amazon's overall Top 20 Best Sellers were self-published.

As of 2016, paper book sales is _____.

Why _____ additional sales?

7. Republish a _____

Out-of-print books are _____ candidates for self-publishing.

8. Other Publishing Options Are Impractical

_____ is part of the game.

There's value in _____.

It's never been easier to _____.

9. Publishing a Book in a _____ Genre

10. Building Your Brand

Becoming a published author can help establish _____.

Self-Reflection

Consider the following questions. Write down your responses in the space provided. These can help guide you and provide insights.

Why do I want to be an author?

What am I most passionate about?

Am I passionate about the subject I'm writing about?

NOTES

Write down any notes, insights or "A-ha!" moments you've had so far.

"And if you've got a writer's block, you can cure it this evening by stopping whatever you're writing and doing something else. You picked the wrong subject."

—*Ray Bradbury*

#MARKTruth

What Do I Write About?

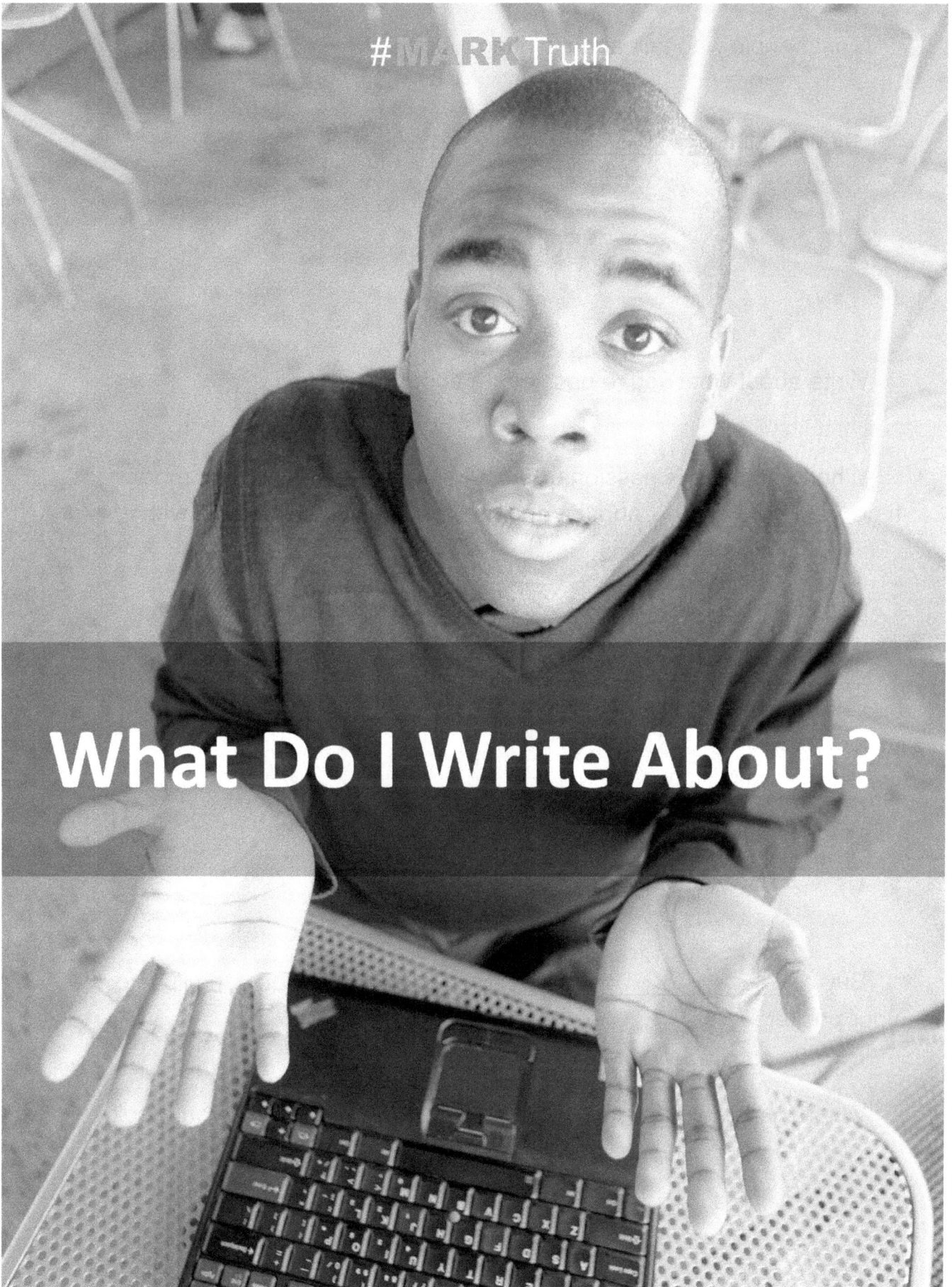

Most people who talk about writing a book _____ _____.

Set aside time _____ _____ to write.

Passion

Write about what you're passionate about.

When someone is passionate about something, they spend more time _____ about it and mastering skills associated with it.

Passion _____ _____ in your writing.

Passion is more likely to lead to _____ _____ than a lack of passion.

I'm Not a Great Writer, But I Can Talk!

Buy a _____ _____ that you can slip into your pocket.

When inspiration hits, pull it out and start _____ your book.

Just _____ your _____.

NOTES

Write down any notes, insights or "A-ha!" moments you've had so far.

"A good editor is like tinsel to a Christmas Tree...they add the perfect amount of sparkle without being gaudy."

—*Bobbi Romans*

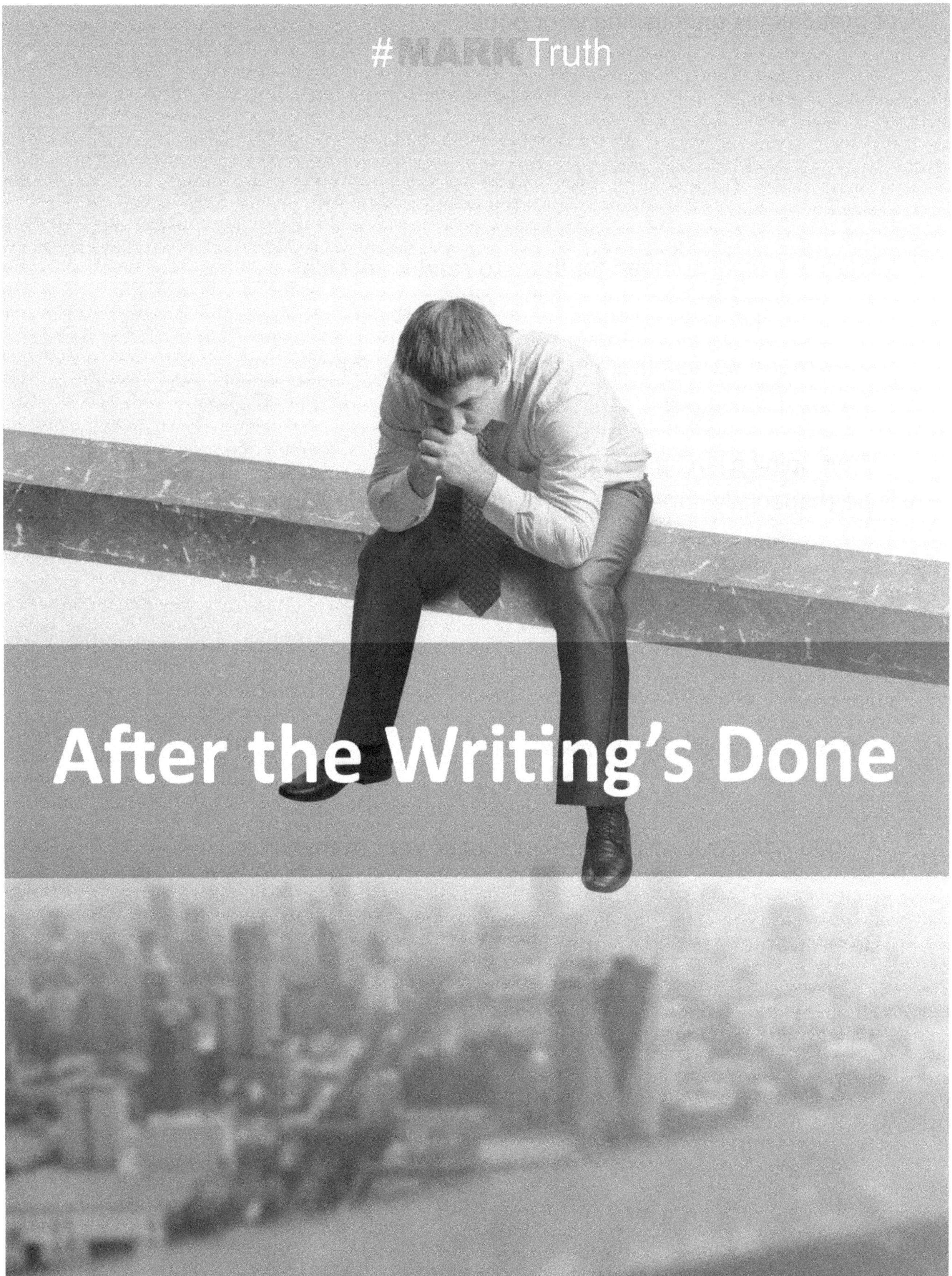
#MARK Truth
After the Writing's Done

Congratulations on finishing your book!

Stay Away from Friends and Family

There's simply no need for them to read it until it's _____.

The reason we ask them in the first place is for _____.

Their opinion isn't a barometer of how _____ your book will be (especially if they aren't your target audience in the first place.

Always Hire an _____

A professional editor: someone who gets _____ to edit manuscripts.

A good editor will redline the hell out of your manuscript.

Be prepared to _____ an editor.

An editor who agrees work for _____ isn't likely to give you 100%.

Word Counts

When you describe your manuscript's length in "pages," you tell professionals that you're an _____.

The industry standard manuscript "page" is _____ words.

Types of Editors

A line editor focuses on the _____ itself rather than on the content in general.

The copy editor improves the _____, _____, and accuracy of text.

Most copy editors who edit in *Word* will use the _____ _____feature.

How to Reduce Editing Costs

Turn over a manuscript that's as _____ as possible.

Basic _____ editing costs less than a substantive edit.

The fewer mistakes an editor has to find and correct, the _____ and smoother the editing process will be.

A novel costs more to edit than a _____ story.

Some editors work on a _____ _____.

If you give your editor a _____ deadline, you're almost guaranteed to pay more for the editing.

A Good Editor Makes You _____

It's human nature not to want to see _____ we've made.

Amateur writers _____ good editing and don't learn from it.

Professional writers _____ from their mistakes and become *better* writers.

NOTES

Write down any notes, insights or "A-ha!" moments you've had so far.

"Since design is important to the eventual success of your book whether you attempt to do it yourself or hire it out, it pays to know something about those conventions and assumptions."

—*Joel Friedlander*

#**MARK**Truth

Book Design

Book design is designing the look of all the elements that make up the _____ of your book.

It's not that a simple design doesn't require work. It simply requires _____ work.

Should I Hire a Book Designer?

You could get away with not hiring a book designer and do your own layout, but there's a _____ _____.

Doing Your Own Book Design

For more advanced designs I prefer to use _____.

Another popular software program is _____.

File Preparation

Most printers accept books submitted in _____ files because they contain everything the printer needs to print the book.

PDF stands for _____ _____ _____.

NOTES

Write down any notes, insights or "A-ha!" moments you've had so far.

"Cover art serves one purpose, and one purpose only, to get potential customers interested long enough to pick up the book to read the back cover blurb. In the internet age that means the thumb nail image needs to be interesting enough to click on. That's what covers are for."

—*Larry Correia*

#MARK Truth

Cover Design

Your book's cover is arguably the _____ _____ part of the book when it comes to sales.

It's generally the _____ that first grabs the buyer's eye.

It's All About Feeling

People make purchases based on _____, then they justify their purchase with _____.

Sometimes Less Is More

A simple image, such as a _____, can achieve invoke an emotion in the viewer as well as a complex painting or illustration, sometimes better.

Hardcover or Paperback?

If you're willing to spend a few extra dollars to produce _____ *copy* of your book, you can publish your book as a hardcover.

Most books are released as _____.

Designing Your Cover

Consider the following questions. Write down your responses in the space provided. These can help guide you and provide insights.

What emotion do I want the cover image to evoke?

What are some iconic images from the genre?

Can a simple image do the job as well as a complex illustration?

What are the pros and cons of hiring a cover designer?

"The greatest book in the world can't be found without an ISBN."

— *Mark T. Arsenault*

#MARK Truth

Don't Forget the ISBN

What's an ISBN?

ISBN stands for International Standards _____ _____.

Since January 1, 2007, ISBNs consist of _____ digits.

Do I Have to Have an ISBN?

ISBNs are the way _____ _____ know how to find and order your book.

Each _____ or version of a book must have a unique ISBN.

How Do I Get an ISBN?

_____ is the sole source for ISBNs for publishers in the United States.

Bowker runs a web site with resources for self-published authors, at http://www.selfpublishedauthor.com.

NOTES

Write down any notes, insights or "A-ha!" moments you've had so far.

"There's nothing like a printed book; the weight, the woody scent, the feel, the look."

— *E.A. Bucchianeri*

#**MARK**Truth

Printing Your Book

Which Format Should I Produce: eBook or Print?

- It's silly to _____ potential sales when the effort to release an eBook is barely more than producing a print edition.
- An eBook edition of your book can open the door to an additional potential _____ _____.
- Notes:

  _____

  _____

  _____

Traditional Printing or POD?

- Traditionally, the cost for printing books was quite _____.
- POD stands for _____ ____ _____.
- The price per copy is _____ than with large runs on a traditional press, but still low enough that a publisher can enjoy a small _____ on even sales of a single copy.
- Notes:

  _____

  _____

  _____

Print on Demand Companies

- The author earns a royalty equal to the wholesale cost of the book minus the _____ cost of the book and any fees.
- LightningSource is owned by _____, the world's largest book distribution company.
- IngramSpark is a _____ version of LightningSource for self-publishing author.
- CreateSpace is _____ POD publishing business.

- Lulu is one of the larger POD book printers, and it claims to have the largest _____ distribution.
- Notes:

_____

_____

_____

POD Production Cost & Royalty Price Comparisons

The following price comparison assumes a single copy of a book sold on Amazon.com with the following specifications: Paperback, 6x9", perfect bound, full color C1S 10-pt cover (or equivalent), B&W printing, white 40# paper, 120 pages, and a retail price of $14.95.

	LightningSource	IngramSpark	CreateSpace	Lulu
Retail Price	$14.99	$14.99	$14.99	$14.99
Wholesale	$6.75	$6.75	N/A	$7.48
Manuf.	$2.67	$2.67	$2.29	$5.50
Fee	$0.00	$0.00	$0.80	$0.40
Royalty	$4.08	$4.08	$6.70	$1.58

"People can't read a book if they don't know it exists. All authors need to do marketing, regardless of how they published."

— *Jo Linsdell*

Marketing

Finding People Who Care

- Nobody cares about your new book unless they _____ about it first.

  _____

  _____

  _____

The Landscape of Marketing Today

- More than _____ of internet views of web pages or social media is done on a smart phone.

  _____

  _____

  _____

Paid Advertising

- The _____ thing I recommend a self-published author do is pay for advertising.
- Facebook ads are one of the best _____ ___

  _____.
- Facebook has 1.59 _____ active users.
- On Twitter you can promote a tweet and use _____ to target viewers who are interested in what you're writing about.

  _____

  _____

  _____

Should I Have a Presence on Social Media?

- If you pick only three social media platforms to participate on, I recommend _____, _____, and _____.

  _____

  _____

  _____

Third Party Social Media Tools

- Third party tools allow you to _____ multiple social media accounts.
- There are apps available that will _____ new users and users who stop following you, _____ send a message to new followers, or all of the above.

  _____

  _____

  _____

Marketing on the Cheap

- There are ways to grow your audience that cost nothing but _____.

  Online Communities:

- Get to know the posting _____ before you start posting.
- Create and nurture _____ with the other users.

  _____

  _____

Business Cards:

- Business cards are inexpensive and make great _____.
- Make the card about _____, not about your _____.
- Use the _____ of the card to include a generic image and a "Thank You!" message.

_____

_____

_____

Classes:

- Even if you don't have a teaching credential, you can be an _____ in a parks and recs class or in a continuing education course.
- Mention being a published author when you _____ yourself.
- At the _____ of the class, it's appropriate to mention your book as a resource for additional information.

_____

_____

_____

Public Speaking:

- You can take speaking to the next level and start speaking to larger groups, such as _____ events, _____ groups, or MeetUp groups, about your topic of choice.
- The host will typically allow you to have a _____ from which to sign – and sell – your books before and after the event.

_____

_____

_____

Guest Writing:

- Writing freelance articles for publications or web sites can be a huge _____ to gaining new fans and readers.

_____

_____

_____

E-mail:

- Every e-mail is a potential advertisement for you, and it isn't considered _____.
- A signature block should clearly and simply communicate _____ I am, _____ I do, and _____ people can get more information about me.

_____

_____

_____

Book Signings:

- If you're a published author, you're a local _____.
- Book signing events are a _____ venture for the store and have a huge upside for you.

_____

_____

_____

Book Trailers:

- You can create a trailer for your _____.

_____

_____

_____

Social Media:

- YouTube is the second largest site used for _____.
- Millions of people are using smartphones and _____ to watch YouTube videos.

_____

_____

_____

Personal Development:

- Personal development has a better _____ than any other single form of investment.
- For every dollar you invest in yourself it returns _____ down the road, in terms of financial success and abundance.
- Read at least ____ minutes (or ____ pages) a day

_____

_____

_____

Press Releases

- Your press release needs to include information about your _____, about _____ and how to _____ you.
- Help the news outlets by writing an interesting _____ for them and they'll be more likely to publish your press release, perhaps verbatim.
- If you're going to do your own press release _____, you'll need to start collecting a list of places to send them to.

_____

_____

_____

Blogging

- Blogging is the most effective means of _____ marketing.
- There are people today receiving thousands of _____ a month from efforts they put into their blogs months or years ago.

Web Hosting:

- _____ is easy to install and makes web site creation as simple as picking elements and clicking your mouse.

_____

_____

_____

Domain Names:

- When registering a _____ _____, try to choose a name that both conveys your brand and is easy to remember.

_____

_____

_____

Give Away Content:

- Providing _____ _____ is the key to gaining followers.
- People do business with those they _____, _____ & _____.

_____

_____

_____

SEO:

- SEO stands for _____ _____ _____.
- Include _____ in your page title and throughout your blog or article.
- If you're running your own _____ _____, start learning SEO.
- If you're using WordPress, consider getting an _____ plug-in.

_____

_____

_____

Be Consistent:

- It's better to post _____ piece of content every week, on schedule, then to sporadically post things with no set schedule.
- Readers should be able to comment on and _____ your blog with their friends on social media.
- Start thinking in terms of _____ _____ _____.
- _____ content is using the content from your blog to create additional content to post on social media platforms.
- _____ with your audience.

_____

_____

_____

Marketing Ideas for Your Book

Consider the following questions. Write down your responses in the space provided. These can help guide you and provide insights.

What are some local businesses I patronize?

What are some ways I can spread the word about my book?

How can I add value to other people in a way that relates to the topic of my book?

List local events I can participate in to raise awareness of my book.

List at least three web sites that relate to my book's topic:

List at least three publications that relate to my book's topic:

List any radio or internet talk shows that give away prizes:

List the top 10 people who should get a free copy of my book:

Who are the top 10 people I wish could see my book?

NOTES

Write down any notes, insights or "A-ha!" moments you've had so far.

"Only one thing is impossible for God: To find any sense in any copyright law on the planet."

—*Mark Twain*

#MARKTruth

Copyrights and Trademarks

This chapter applies to _____ copyright law.

What is copyright?

- According to the U.S. Copyright Office, "Copyright is a form of protection granted by law for original _____ of authorship fixed in a _____ medium of expression."
- "Copyright" is essentially the _____ to make _____.

What does copyright protect?

- Anything you create and "express" through some _____ and perceivable form can be protected.
- Copyright does not protect _____, _____, systems, or methods of operation...

How is a copyright different from a patent or a trademark?

- Copyright protects original works of authorship, while a patent protects _____ or _____.

Let's look at a bottle of Nutty Cola.

- The original recipe or "**formula**" for the Nutty Cola drink can be _____ as an invention.
- The **written expression** of the formula (but not the formula itself) would be protected by _____.
- The "Nutty Cola" **name & logo** would be a _____ (if used on packaging, advertising, etc.).

When is my work protected?

- Your work is under copyright protection the moment it is _____ and fixed in a _____ form that it is perceptible either directly or with the aid of a machine or device (source: copyright.gov).
- "Copyright" is a _____, not a _____.
- You must _____ your copyright with the U.S. Copyright Office to file a lawsuit for copyright infringement, get a court order to stop someone from making and distributing copies of your work, or to collect damages.

Do I have to register with the Copyright Office to be protected?

- Registration of your copyright is _____.

Why register if copyright protection is automatic?

- Registering your work provides you with a _____ of registration.
- Registered works may be eligible for statutory _____ and attorney's fees in a successful lawsuit.
- Registration of your copyright within _____ years of publication is considered *prime facie* evidence in court (a rebuttable presumption that you are the copyright holder).

What is a Trademark?

- A trademark is a _____ name.
- A trademark or _____ mark includes any word, name, symbol, device, or any combination, used or intended to be used to identify and distinguish the _____/services of one _____ or provider from those of others.

NOTES

Write down any notes, insights or "A-ha!" moments you've had so far.

www.ingramcontent.com/pod-product-compliance
Lightning Source LLC
Chambersburg PA
CBHW080004280326
41935CB00013B/1748